A Change of Heart

A Change of Heart

A Story for Women About the Mother-in-Law Relationship,
Including an Eight-Week Study that Will
Change Your Heart

Andrea Evans
Margaret Miller
Janie Putman

Rutledge Books, Inc.

Danbury, CT

ALL RIGHTS RESERVED
Rutledge Books, Inc.
107 Mill Plain Road, Danbury, CT 06811
1-800-278-8533
www.rutledgebooks.com
Author photo by Evan Miller

Manufactured in the United States of America

Cataloging in Publication Data
Evans, Andrea, Miller, Margaret, and Putman, Janie
    A Change of Heart

    ISBN: 1-58244-241-X

    1. Relationships: mother-in-law/daughter-in-law

Library of Congress Catalog Card Number: 2002114529

For our mothers-in-law
Jane, June Elizabeth, and Lucy

Table of Contents

Longing For Love

Introduction

Our quest for a better understanding of the relationship between a mother-in-law and daughter-in-law began with a Christmas trip that Andrea and her husband, Max, were planning to take to visit his parents in Ohio. The holiday trip had become part of their family's tradition. This time, however, was different. For the first time in their marriage, Andrea expressed a reluctance to go, and Max was frustrated and hurt.

Prayer and insight into her feelings helped Andrea begin to understand the reason behind her hesitation. While Andrea respected Max's mother, Jane had often seemed like "the other woman" in Andrea's marriage. In other words, Jane was tied to Max in an intimate way and Andrea was expected to love and accept her even though she had not "chosen" her—just as Jane had not "chosen" Andrea. Despite these underlying issues, Andrea longed for something more in her relationship with her mother-in-law.

When Andrea shared her feelings and experiences with us (Margaret and Janie), we immediately identified with them. It became clear to us that the mother-in-law relationship was a significant aspect of every married woman's life which was very personal and complex and often problematic. A visit to local bookstores and libraries confirmed our suspicion that it had not been explored in as much depth as other issues relating to marriage.

Pursuing our interest, we sent a questionnaire to 200 friends and acquaintances which examined the mother-in-law/daughter-in-law relationship and gave women an opportunity to reflect on their experiences. It soon became clear that there was a desire and a need for more information and support regarding this important relationship.

Differences in temperaments can make accepting one another very difficult. Forgiving one another, asking for help, and reaching a place of peace can seem impossible. Yet, through perseverance, by faith in Christ, a change of heart is possible, despite seemingly overwhelming circumstances.

Three close friends put this book together, each contributing her own gifts and insights. Each of us has experienced this miraculous change through faith and persistence in our relationships with the woman who gave birth to the men we fell in love with. It's our hearts' desire that every woman enjoy a relationship with her mother-in-law that is as fulfilling as possible and that we will learn to be godly mothers-in-law ourselves, if that role is in our future.

Beginning Your Change of Heart

Our book is presented in three parts. Part One offers a unique way for you to "look in the mirror" and understand the way you see others through a questionnaire about your relationship with your mother-in-law and a unique personality test designed by Florence Littauer. Both will give you valuable insights into your own personality and temperament. Part Two presents the fictional journal of a woman who, like most of us, has wrestled with the many roles a woman undertakes throughout her life. The stories in the journal are derived from the over-200 mothers-in-law and daughters-in-law who responded to our questionnaire. While every experience is unique, it's our prayer that Mary Beth's narrative will address many of the common challenges that women face in their relationships and provide insightful, practical ways to foster acceptance and improve communication.

In Part Three, you'll follow a guided study plan that will allow you to reflect on your own life situation and look to the Bible for guidance and healing in your relationships—even if the situations and people around you do not change. The blank journal pages included at the end of this book provide a personal space for you to record your thoughts, feelings, and progress as you work on your relationships.

We hope that each woman who reads this book will embark on her change of heart with patience and persistence. While each part is important, we believe that the Bible study is the key to success in making peace within a troubled relationship. The Bible is a powerful tool which can equip each of us to make significant changes in our lives, our relationships and ourselves. Most of us have learned how difficult such changes can be. But we've been assured that with God's help, all things are possible.

"Now to Him who is able to do exceedingly abundantly beyond all that we ask or think, according to the power that works within us . . ." (Ephesians 3:20)

Andrea Evans, Margaret Miller, Janie Putman

Twenty Questions For Daughters-in-Law

1. Is your husband an only child?   yes   no

   If not, what is the birth order of his brothers and sisters?

   _____

2. How old were you at the time of your marriage? _____

   How old was your mother-in-law? _____

3. How old are you now? _____

   How old is she? _____

4. How long did you know her before you were married? _____

5. Did you feel accepted by her during that time? _____

6. Do you talk easily and honestly with her? _____

7. How do you address your mother-in-law? _____

   How does she address you? _____

8. a. Do you have similar educational backgrounds?   yes   no

   b. Do you have similar religious beliefs?   yes   no

   c. Does she generally share your values?   yes   no

   d. If there is a difference in the above areas, do any of these

      differences matter to you? Which ones, and why? _____

   _____

9. Do you believe that your mother-in-law thinks that you have made

   your son happy?   yes   no   I don't know

10. Are you her only daughter-in-law?   yes   no

If not, describe any differences you perceive in the ways your mother-in-law relates to you and to your sisters-in-law. _____

_____

11. Does your mother-in-law have characteristics or habits which are irritating to you? (for example, she talks too much, knows all the answers, curses, smokes, drinks, is meddlesome, or other bothersome traits) If so, how do you handle the irritations?

_____

_____

12. Have feelings of anger between you continued to build over the years, or are hurt feelings settled? _____

_____

13. If you have children, does she agree with your way of handling and disciplining them? Explain how having children has affected your relationship with your mother-in-law? _____

_____

_____

14. Is it a consideration that your mother-in-law may live with you someday? Why or why not? _____

_____

15. Describe three things that make the mother/daughter-in-law relationship difficult. _____

_____

16. Describe three things that your mother-in-law has done which have contributed to family harmony. _____

_____

_____

17. Seeing her as a role model, what have you learned that you want to <u>avoid</u> in your own daughter-in-law/mother-in-law relationship? _____

_____

18. Did you like your mother-in-law right away, later, or never? How have your feelings for her changed over the years? _____

_____

_____

19. Describe the characteristics of your mother-in-law which you admire? _____

_____

20. Describe the most memorable experience you and your mother-in-law have shared—positive or negative—and explain how it has affected your relationship. _____

_____

_____

LITTAUER PERSONALITY TEST

PERSONALITY PROFILE
Created by Fred Littauer

DIRECTIONS: In each of the following rows of four words across, place an X in front of the one word that most often applies to you. Continue through all forty lines. Be sure each number Is marked. If you are not sure of which word "most applies," ask a spouse or a friend, and think of what your answer would have been when you were a child.

STRENGTHS

1	Adventurous		Adaptable		Animated		Analytical
2	Persistent		Playful		Persuasive		Peaceful
3	Submissive		Self-sacrificing		Sociable		Strong-willed
4	Considerate		Controlled		Competitive		Convincing
5	Refreshing		Respectful		Reserved		Resourceful
6	Satisfied		Sensitive		Self-reliant		Spirited
7	Planner		Patient		Positive		Promoter
8	Sure		Spontaneous		Scheduled		Shy
9	Orderly		Obliging		Outspoken		Optimistic
10	Friendly		Faithful		Funny		Forceful
11	Daring		Delightful		Diplomatic		Detailed
12	Cheerful		Consistent		Cultured		Confident
13	Idealistic		Independent		Inoffensive		Inspiring
14	Demonstrative		Decisive		Dry humor		Deep
15	Mediator		Musical		Mover		Mixes easily
16	Thoughtful		Tenacious		Talker		Tolerant
17	Listener		Loyal		Leader		Lively
18	Contented		Chief		Chartmaker		Cute
19	Perfectionist		Pleasant		Productive		Popular
20	Bouncy		Bold		Behaved		Balanced

WEAKNESSES

Reprinted by permission from PERSONALITY PLUS, Florence Littauer, Fleming H. Revell Publishers. All Rights Reserved

21	Blank		Bashful		Brassy		Bossy
22	Undisciplined		Unsympathetic		Unenthusiastic		Unforgiving
23	Reticent		Resentful		Resistant		Repetitious
24	Fussy		Fearful		Forgetful		Frank
25	Impatient		Insecure		Indecisive		Interrupts
26	Unpopular		Uninvolved		Unpredictable		Unaffectionate
27	Headstrong		Haphazard		Hard to please		Hesitant
28	Plain		Pessimistic		Proud		Permissive
29	Angered easily		Aimless		Argumentative		Alienated
30	Naive		Negative attitude		Nervy		Nonchalant
31	Worrier		Withdrawn		Workaholic		Wants credit
32	Too sensitive		Tactless		Timid		Talkative
33	Doubtful		Disorganized		Domineering		Depressed
34	Inconsistent		Introvert		Intolerant		Indifferent
35	Messy		Moody		Mumbles		Manipulative
36	Slow		Stubborn		Show-off		Skeptical
37	Loner		Lord over		Lazy		Loud
38	Sluggish		Suspicious		Short-tempered		Scatterbrained
39	Revengeful		Restless		Reluctant		Rash
40	Compromising		Critical		Crafty		Changeable

NOW TRANSFER ALL YOUR X'S TO THE CORRESPONDING WORDS ON THE PERSONALITY SCORING SHEET AND ADD UP YOUR TOTALS.

Personality Test Word Definitions
(Adapted From Personality Patterns by Lana Bateman)

STRENGTHS

1.	ADVENTUROUS	-One who will take on new and daring enterprises a determination to master them.
	ADAPTABLE	-Easily fits and is comfortable in any situation!
	ANIMATED	-Full of life, lively use of hand, arm, and face gestures.
	ANALYTICAL	-Likes to examine the parts for their logical and proper relationships.
2.	PERSISTENT	-Sees one project through to its completion before starting another.
	PLAYFUL	-Full of fun and good humor.
	PERSUASIVE	-Convinces through logic and fact rather than charm or power.
	PEACEFUL	-Seems undisturbed and tranquil and retreats from any form of strife.
3.	SUBMISSIVE	-Easily accepts any other's point of view or desire with little need to assert his own opinion.
	SELF-	-Willingly gives up his own personal being for the sake of, or to meet the needs of others.
	SOCIABLE	-One who sees being with others as an Opportunity to be cute and entertaining rather than as a challenge or business opportunity.
	STRONG- WILLED	-One who is determined to have his own way.
4.	CONSIDERATE	-Having regard for the needs and feelings of others.
	CONTROLLED	-Has emotional feelings but rarely displays them.
	COMPETITIVE	-Turns every situation, happening, or game into a contest and always plays to win!
	CONVINCING	-Can win you over to anything through the 1heer charm of his personality.
5.	REFRESHING	-Renews and stimulates or makes others feel good.
	RESPECTFUL	-Treats others with deference, honor, and esteem.
	RESERVED	-Self restraint in expression of emotion or enthusiasm.
	RESOURCEFUL	-Able to act quickly and effectively in virtually all situations.
6.	SATISFIED	-A person who easily accepts any circumstance or situation.
	SENSITIVE	-Intensively cares about others, and what happens.
	SELF-RELIANT	-An independent person who can fully rely on his own capabilities, judgment, and resources.
	SPIRITED	-Full of life and excitement.
7.	PLANNER	-Prefers to work out a detailed arrangement beforehand, for the accomplishment of project or goal, and prefers involvement with the planning stages and the finished product rather than the carrying out of the task.
	PATIENT	-Unmoved by delay, remains calm and tolerant.
	POSITIVE	-Knows it will turn out right if he's in charge.
	PROMOTER	-Urges or compels others to go along, join, or invest through the charm of his own personality.
8.	SURE	-Confident, rarely hesitates or wavers.
	SPONTANEOUS	-Prefers all of life to be impulsive, unpremeditated activity, not restricted by plans.
	SCHEDULED	-Makes, and lives, according to a daily plan, dislikes his plan to be interrupted.
	SHY	-Quiet, doesn't easily instigate a conversation.
9.	ORDERLY	-A person who has a methodical, systematic arrangement of things.
	OBLIGING	-Accommodating. One who is quick to do it another's way.
	OUTSPOKEN	-Speaks frankly and without reserve.
	OPTIMISTIC	-Sunny disposition who convinces himself and others that everything will turn out all right.
10.	FRIENDLY	-A responder rather than an initiator, seldom starts a conversation.
	FAITHFUL	-Consistently reliable, steadfast, loyal, and devoted sometimes beyond reason.
	FUNNY	-Sparkling sense of humor that can make virtually any story into an hilarious event.
	FORCEFUL	-A commanding personality whom others would hesitate to take a stand against.
11.	DARING	-Willing to take risks; fearless, bold.
	DELIGHTFUL	-A person who is upbeat and fun to be with.
	DIPLOMATIC	-Deals with people tactfully, sensitively, and patiently.
	DETAILED	-Does everything in proper order with a clear memory of all the things that happened.
12.	CHEERFUL	-Consistently in good spirits and promoting happiness in others.
	CONSISTENT	-Stays emotionally on an even keel, responding as one might expect.
	CULTURED	-One whose interests involve both intellectual and artistic pursuits, such as theatre, symphony, ballet.
	CONFIDENT	-Self-assured and certain of own ability and success.

13.	IDEALISTIC	-Visualizes things in their perfect form, and has a need to measure up to that standard himself.
	INDEPENDENT	-Self-sufficient, self-supporting, self-confident and seems to have little need of help.
	INOFFENSIVE	-A person who never says or causes anything unpleasant or objectionable.
	INSPIRING	-Encourages others to work, join, or be involved and makes the whole thing fun.
14.	DEMONSTRATIVE	-Openly expresses emotion, especially affection and doesn't hesitate to touch others while speaking to them.
	DECISIVE	-A person with quick, conclusive, judgment-making ability.
	DRY HUMOR	-Exhibits "dry wit", usually humorous one-liners which can be sarcastic in nature.
	DEEP	-Intense and often introspective with a distaste for surface conversation and pursuits.
15.	MEDIATOR	-Consistently finds himself in the role of reconciling differences in order to avoid conflict.
	MUSICAL	-Participates in or has a deep appreciation for music, is committed to music as an art form, rather than the fun of performance.
	MOVER	-Driven by a need to be productive, is a leader whom others follow, finds it difficult to sit still.
	MIXES EASILY	-Loves a party and can't wait to meet everyone in the room, never meets a stranger.
16.	THOUGHTFUL	-A considerate person who remembers special occasions and is quick to make a kind gesture.
	TENACIOUS	-Holds on firmly, stubbornly, and won't let go until the goal is accomplished.
	TALKER	-Constantly talking, generally telling funny stories and entertaining everyone around, feeling the need to fill the silence in order to make others comfortable.
	TOLERANT	-Easily accepts the thoughts and ways of others without the need to disagree with or change them.
17.	LISTENER	-Always seems willing to hear what you have to say.
	LOYAL	-Faithful to a person, ideal, or job, sometimes beyond reason.
	LEADER	-A natural born director, who is driven to be in charge, and often finds it difficult to believe that anyone else can do the job as well.
	LIVELY	-Full of life, vigorous, energetic.
18.	CONTENTED	-Easily satisfied with what he has, rarely envious.
	CHIEF	-Commands leadership and expects people to follow.
	CHARTMAKER	-Organizes life, tasks, and problem solving by making lists, forms or graphs.
	CUTE	-Precious, adorable, center of attention.
19.	PERFECTIONIST	-Places high standards on himself, and often on others, desiring that everything be in proper order at all times.
	PLEASANT	-Easy going, easy to be around, easy to talk with.
	PRODUCTIVE	-Must constantly be working or achieving, often finds it very difficult to rest.
	POPULAR	-Life of the party and therefore much desired as a party guest.
20.	BOUNCY	-A bubbly, lively personality, full of energy.
	BOLD	-Fearless, daring, forward, unafraid of risk.
	BEHAVED	-Consistently desires to conduct himself within the realm of what he feels is proper.
	BALANCED	-Stable, middle of the road personality, not subject to sharp highs or lows.

WEAKNESSES

21.	BLANK	-A person who shows little facial expression or emotion.
	BASHFUL	-Shrinks from getting attention, resulting from self-consciousness.
	BRASSY	-Showy, flashy, comes on strong, too loud.
	BOSSY	-Commanding, domineering, sometimes overbearing in adult relationships.
22.	UNDISCIPLINED	-A person whose lack or order permeates most every area of his life.
	UNSYMPATHETIC	-Finds it difficult to relate to the problems or hurts of others.
	UNENTHUSIASTIC	-Tends to not get excited, often feeling it won't work anyway.
	UNFORGIVING	-One who has difficulty releasing or forgetting a hurt or injustice done to them, apt to hold onto a grudge.
23.	RETICENT	-Unwilling or struggles against getting involved,especially when complex.
	RESENTFUL	-Often holds ill feelings as a result of real or imagined offenses.
	RESISTANT	-Strives, works against, or hesitates to accept any other way but his own.
	REPETITIOUS	-Retells stories and incidents to entertain you without realizing he has already told the story several times before, is constantly needing something to say.
24.	FUSSY	-Insistent over petty matters or details, calling for great attention to trivial details.
	FEARFUL	-Often experiences feelings of deep concern,apprehension or anxiousness.
	FORGETFUL	-Lack of memory which is usually tied to a lack of discipline and not bothering to mentally record things that aren't fun.
	FRANK	-Straightforward, outspoken, and doesn't mind telling you exactly what he thinks.
25.	IMPATIENT	-A person who finds it difficult to endure irritation or wait for others.

	INSECURE	-One who is apprehensive or lacks confidence.
	INDECISIVE	-The person who finds it difficult to make any decision at all. (Not the personality that labors long over each decision in order to make the perfect one.)
	INTERRUPTS	-A person who is more of a talker than a listener, who starts speaking without even realizing someone else is already speaking.
26.	UNPOPULAR	-A person whose intensity and demand for perfection can push others away.
	UNINVOLVED	-Has no desire to listen or become interested in clubs, groups, activities, or other people's lives.
	UNPREDICTABLE	-May be ecstatic one moment and down the next, or willing to help but then disappears, or promises to come but forgets to show up.
	UNAFFECTIONATE	-Finds it difficult to verbally or physically demonstrate tenderness openly.
27.	HEADSTRONG	-Insists on having his own way.
	HAPHAZARD	-Has no consistent way of doing things.
	HARD TO PLEASE	-A person whose standards are set so high that it is difficult to ever satisfy them.
	HESITANT	-Slow to get moving and hard to get involved.
28.	PLAIN	-A middle-of-the road personality without highs or lows and showing little, if any, emotion.
	PESSIMISTIC	-While hoping for the best, this person generally sees the down side of a situation first.
	PROUD	-One with great self-esteem who sees himself as always right and the best person for the job.
	PERMISSIVE	-Allows others (including children) to do as they please in order to keep from being disliked
29.	ANGERED EASILY	-One who has a childlike flash-in-the-pan temper that expresses itself in tantrum style and is over and forgotten almost instantly.
	AIMLESS	-Not a goal-setter with little desire to be one.
	ARGUMENTATIVE	-Incites arguments generally because he is certain he is right no matter what the situation may be.
	ALIENATED	-Easily feels estranged from others often because of insecurity or fear that others don't really enjoy his company.
30.	NAIVE	-Simple and child-like perspective, lacking sophistication or comprehension of what the deeper levels of life are really about.
	NEGATIVE	-One whose attitude is seldom positive and is often able to see only the down or dark side of each.
	NERVY	-Full of confidence, fortitude, and sheer guts, often in a negative sense.
	NONCHALANT	-Easy-going, unconcerned, indifferent.
31.	WORRIER	-Consistently feels uncertain, troubled, or anxious.
	WITHDRAWN	-A person who pulls back to himself and needs a great deal of alone or isolation time.
	WORKAHOLIC	-An aggressive goal-setter who must be constantly productive and feels very guilty when resting, is not driven by a need for perfection or completion but by a need for accomplishment and reward.
	WANTS CREDIT	-Thrives on the credit or approval of others. As an entertainer this person feeds on the applause, laughter, and/or acceptance of an audience.
32.	TOO SENSITIVE	-Overly introspective and easily offended when misunderstood.
	TACTLESS	-Sometimes expresses himself in a somewhat offensive and inconsiderate way.
	TIMID	-Shrinks from difficult situations
	TALKATIVE	-An entertaining, compulsive talker who finds it difficult to listen.
33.	DOUBTFUL	-Characterized by uncertainty and lack or lack of confidence that it will ever work out.
	DISORGANIZED	-Lack of ability to ever get life in order.
	DOMINEERING	-Compulsively takes control of situations and/or people, usually telling others what to do.
	DEPRESSED	-A person who feels down much of the time.
34.	INCONSISTENT	-Erratic, contradictory, with actions and emotions not based on logic.
	INTROVERT	-A person whose thoughts and interest are directed inward, lives within himself.
	INTOLERANT	-Appears unable to withstand or accept another's attitudes, point of view or way of doing things.
	INDIFFERENT	-A person to whom most things don't matter one way or the other.
35.	MESSY	-Living in a state of disorder, unable to find things.
	MOODY	-Doesn't get very high emotionally, but easily slips into low lows, often when feeling unappreciated.
	MUMBLES	-Will talk quietly under the breath when pushed. Doesn't bother to speak clearly.
	MANIPULATIVE	-Influences or manages shrewdly or deviously for his own advantage, will get his way somehow.
36.	SLOW	-Doesn't often act or think quickly, too much bother.
	STUBBORN	-Determined to exert his own will, not easily persuaded, obstinate.
	SHOW-OFF	-Needs to be the center of attention, wants to be watched.
	SKEPTICAL	-Disbelieving, questioning the motive behind the words.
37.	LONER	-Requires a lot of private time and tends to avoid other people.
	LORD OVER	-Doesn't hesitate to let you know that he is right or is in control.
	LAZY	-Evaluates work or activity in terms of how much energy it will take.
	LOUD	-A person whose laugh or voice can be heard above others in the room.
38.	SLUGGISH	-Slow to get started, needs push to be motivated.
	SUSPICIOUS	-Tends to suspect or distrust others or ideas.
	SHORT-TEMPERED	-Has a demanding impatience-based anger and a short fuse. Anger is expressed when others are not moving fast enough or have not completed what they have been asked to do.

	SCATTER-BRAINED	-Lacks the power of concentration or attention, flighty.
39.	REVENGEFUL	-Knowingly or otherwise holds the offender, often by subtly withholding friendship or affection.
	RESTLESS	-Likes constant new activity because it isn't fun to do the same things all the time.
	RELUCTANT	-Unwilling or struggles against getting involved.
	RASH	-May act hastily, without thinking things through, generally because of impatience.
40.	COMPROMISING	-Will often relax his position, even when right, in order to avoid conflict.
	CRITICAL	-Constantly evaluating and making judgments, frequently thinking or expressing negative reactions.
	CRAFTY	-Shrewd, one who can always find a way to get to the desired end.
	CHANGEABLE	-A child-like, short attention span that needs a change and variety to keep from getting bored.

15

Having transferred your checked words from the "Profile", page 1, to the scoring sheet on page 4, you should now have a pattern of your Personality. Be sure to subtotal each column separately for strengths and for weaknesses.

Natural combinations of birth personalities are:
Popular Sanguine/Powerful Choleric
Powerful Choleric/Perfect Melancholy
Peaceful Phlegmatic/Popular Sanguine
Perfect Melancholy/Peaceful. Phlegmatic
One of the two will be your dominant and the other will be your secondary. Most everyone has a dominant and a secondary, but the numbers may vary greatly. For example 32 Powerful Choleric with 8 Perfect Melancholy would be described as a very strong Powerful Choleric

with some Perfect Melancholy traits. However, it is also quite possible to have more evenly balanced scores in two columns. A few checks in the remaining two columns can generally be ignored as insignificant. Any test such as this can be assumed to have a ten percent margin of error, for the words simply represent how you perceive yourself. Normal healthy patterns are usually characterized by similar and balancing scores of strengths and weaknesses in any single column.

There are two combinations, though often seen, that are not natural:
1. Popular Sanguine/Perfect Melancholy, and 2. Powerful Choleric/Peaceful Phlegmatic. Either of these two appearing on the scoring sheet in significant numbers is evidence of either a "misunderstanding" or a "personality mask" as they are diametrically opposite and are not natural birth personality combinations. To determine your true Personality, review the Profile again. First, make sure that you used the word definitions for each and every word selection. Additionally, be sure that you selected the words that represent your true, natural self before you worked at becoming a more mature, better person. For example, if you are organized, but it is something you have made a conscious effort to achieve rather than something you have been all your life, do not check organized. Basically, if you

have "learned" it, do not check it. Second, go back over each grouping or words. If you had a difficult time choosing between two words, now check both words. If none of the words seemed appropriate, skip that line. While this approach will adjust the totals so that they do not add up to the usual forty, it will give a more accurate profile and usually clears up any confusion on the Personality pattern. However, if this approach still produces an unnatural combination, it may be indicative of a "personality mask." They are inevitably (1) the result of outside forces working in our life to make us conform to someone else's concept of who we should be or (2) put on in childhood to survive in a difficult or dysfunctional family living situation. If a "personality mask" is present, reading **Freeing Your Mind** is suggested.

1. **A domineering parent** in childhood, constantly requiring the child to conform to the personality they want the child to have. A Perfect Melancholy/Powerful Choleric parent, for example, tries to make a spontaneous Popular Sanguine child into a meticulously neat Perfect Melancholy.

2. An **alcoholic parent** in childhood, forcing unnatural pressures for the child to perform. or contribute to the household, often assuming parental roles not natural for a child or his God-given birth personality.

3. Strong **rejection feelings** in childhood. When a child who does not feel the love of one parent, especially true if it is both parents. The child will often try to "be perfect" for the unloving parent in order to win the love, attention, and approval so eagerly craved and needed by every child.

4. Any form of **emotional or physical abuse** will quickly teach the child that the only way to hope to stop the harsh treatment is to conform to the demands of the abusing parent.

5. **Childhood sexual interference** or violation is inevitably a cause of masking, pa.particularly when perpetrated by a parent or a person playing the parental role. The child subconsciously rationalizes that maybe if I would just be good enough, they would leave me alone. This is especially true when the knowledge of these childhood experiences has been completely suppressed and unknown in adult life. This mask may be seen in a person with a high score in Perfect Melancholy weaknesses, without a comparable number of strengths; or in a person with a high number of Popular Sanguine strengths without balancing weaknesses.

6. **Single Parent Home**. A child raised in a single parent home, especially a first Born, may often be required to fulfill some o the roles of the absent parent. When these functions are not consistent with the child's natural personality, he is apt to put on a mask that he generally continues wearing in adult life.

7. **Birth Order**. Young parents frequently pour on their first child an overzealous energy to make that child conform to their concept of what he/she should be. When this does not coincide with the natural personality masking may result.

8. **Legalistic Religious Home**. Intensely regulatory standards where appearance and conformance are required will often throttle a child's natural personality and zest for living, as the child learns to conform to legalism rather than respond to love.

9. A **domineering and controlling spouse** in adult life can have a similar effect as a domineering parent in childhood. This is most often seen, for example, when a strong Perfect Melancholy/Powerful Choleric husband tries to change a Popular Sanguine wife Into his concept of what his wife should be, and how she should act. After a period of such control she may perceive herself to be Perfect Melancholy/Peaceful Phlegmatic, when in fact it is nothing more than a mask to cope or survive in the marriage.

10. **Adult abuse or rejection** in marriage will often have the same effect in distorting the natural personality, as the lonely or hurting person puts on a mask and simply gives up.

Any combination of three Personalities indicates one must be a mask, for the reasons described above. Generally, the "center" of the three is the natural, one of the "ends" is a mask. For example, for a person scoring relatively evenly in Popular Sanguine/Powerful Choleric/Perfect Melancholy, the Powerful Choleric is the mask, as you were not born with both. You should try to determine which is the real and which is the mask.

Frequently a person who knows you well can objectively review and your two columns in question and help you better select the word that they feel describes you better. Or, you can think back to how you felt or would have answered as a child before life's experiences distorted your perception generally the natural and either the Popular Sanguine or the Perfect Melancholy is of yourself. Such a review of the words you selected will frequently transfer enough of them to another column to clearly define your correct and natural birth personalities. See instructions in "Unnatural Combinations."

UNNATURAL COMBINATIONS

When your profile scores are fairly even across, there are two possibilities. One, you really don't know yourself and probably don't care; or you are Phlegmatic, it doesn't matter, and you have trouble making choices. Or, two, you are "double masked". The way you perceive yourself has been so distorted by life's experiences that you really don't know who you are. Refer to the Causes of Masking to see if any apply to you.

Remember, It takes a great deal of energy to wear a mask and live in a personality role that is not naturally yours. Our goal should be to take off the mask and live life to the fullest for which God created us.

CAUSES OF MASKING

1. To understand your own Personality strengths and weakness: **Personality Plus**, Florence Littauer, Fleming H. Revell Co.
2. To understand masking: **Your Personality Tree**, Florence Littauer, Word.
3. To understand effects of childhood trauma: **Freeing Your Mind from Memories that Bind**, Fred & Florence Littauer, and **The Promise of Healing**, Fred Littauer, Thomas Nelson Publishers.
4. To understand children's Personalities: **Raising Christians, Not Just Children**, Florence Littauer, Word.
5. To understand your leadership potential: **Put Power in Your Personality**, Florence Littauer, Fleming H. Revell Co. Publishers.

6. To understand the Personality of others, especially in the workplace: **Personality Puzzle**, Florence Littauer & Marita L Revell Co.
7. To apply the teaching on the Personalities to various aspects of life such as marriage, parenting, church and spiritual life, even friends and shopping: **Getting Along With Almost Anybody**, Florence Littauer &. Marita Littauer, Freming H. Revell Co.
8. To learn how your Personality shapes your relationship with God. **Come As You Are**, Marita Littauer & Betty Southard, Bethany House

PERSONALITY SCORING SHEET

NAME_____

STRENGTHS

		SANGUINE POPULAR	CHOLERIC POWERFUL	MELANCHOLY PERFECT	PHLEGMATIC PEACEFUL
1		___ Animated	___ Adventurous	___ Analytical	___ Adaptable
2		___ Playful	___ Persuasive	___ Persistent	___ Peaceful
3		___ Sociable	___ Strong-willed	___ Self-sacrificing	___ Submissive
4		___ Convincing	___ Competitive	___ Considerate	___ Controlled
5		___ Refreshing	___ Resourceful	___ Respectful	___ Reserved
6		___ Spirited	___ Self-reliant	___ Sensitive	___ Satisfied
7		___ Promoter	___ Positive	___ Planner	___ Patient
8		___ Spontaneous	___ Sure	___ Scheduled	___ Shy
9		___ Optimistic	___ Outspoken	___ Orderly	___ Obliging
10		___ Funny	___ Forceful	___ Faithful	___ Friendly
11		___ Delightful	___ Daring	___ Detailed	___ Diplomatic
12		___ Cheerful	___ Confident	___ Cultured	___ Consistent
13		___ Inspiring	___ Independent	___ Idealistic	___ Inoffensive
14		___ Demonstrative	___ Decisive	___ Deep	___ Dry humor
15		___ Mixes easily	___ Mover	___ Musical	___ Mediator
16		___ Talker	___ Tenacious	___ Thoughtful	___ Tolerant
17		___ Lively	___ Leader	___ Loyal	___ Listener
18		___ Cute	___ Chief	___ Chartmaker	___ Contented
19		___ Popular	___ Productive	___ Perfectionist	___ Pleasant
20		___ Bouncy	___ Bold	___ Behaved	___ Balanced

SUBTOTALS ___   ___   ___   ___

WEAKNESSES

		SANGUINE	CHOLERIC	MELANCHOLY	PHLEGMATIC
21		___ Brassy	___ Bossy	___ Bashful	___ Blank
22		___ Undisciplined	___ Unsympathetic	___ Unforgiving	___ Unenthusiastic
23		___ Repetitious	___ Resistant	___ Resentful	___ Reticent
24		___ Forgetful	___ Frank	___ Fussy	___ Fearful
25		___ Interrupts	___ Impatient	___ Insecure	___ Indecisive
26		___ Unpredictable	___ Unaffectionate	___ Unpopular	___ Uninvolved
27		___ Haphazard	___ Headstrong	___ Hard-to-please	___ Hesitant
28		___ Permissive	___ Proud	___ Pessimistic	___ Plain
29		___ Angered easily	___ Argumentative	___ Alienated	___ Aimless
30		___ Naive	___ Nervy	___ Negative attitude	___ Nonchalant
31		___ Wants credit	___ Workaholic	___ Withdrawn	___ Worrier
32		___ Talkative	___ Tactless	___ Too sensitive	___ Timid
33		___ Disorganized	___ Domineering	___ Depressed	___ Doubtful
34		___ Inconsistent	___ Intolerant	___ Introverted	___ Indifferent
35		___ Messy	___ Manipulative	___ Moody	___ Mumbles
36		___ Show-off	___ Stubborn	___ Skeptical	___ Slow
37		___ Loud	___ Lord-over-others	___ Loner	___ Lazy
38		___ Scatterbrained	___ Short tempered	___ Suspicious	___ Sluggish
39		___ Restless	___ Rash	___ Revengeful	___ Reluctant
40		___ Changeable	___ Crafty	___ Critical	___ Compromising

SUBTOTALS ___   ___   ___   ___

GRAND ___   ___   ___   ___
TOTAL

STRENGTHS

	SANGUINE-POPULAR	CHOLERIC-POWERFUL	MELANCHOLY-PERFECT	PHLEGMATIC-PEACEFUL
E M O T I O N S	Appealing personality Talkative, storyteller Life of the party Good sense of humor Memory for color Physically holds on to listener Emotional and demonstrative Enthusiastic and expressive Cheerful and bubbling over Curious Good on stage Wide-eyed and innocent Lives in the present Changeable disposition Sincere at heart Always a child	Born leader Dynamic and active Compulsive need for change Must correct wrongs Strong-willed and decisive Unemotional Not easily discouraged Independent and self-sufficient Exudes confidence Can run anything	Deep and thoughtful Analytical Serious and purposeful Genius prone Talented and creative Artistic or musical Philosophical and poetic Appreciative of beauty Sensitive to others Self-sacrificing Conscientious Idealistic	Low-key personality Easygoing and relaxed Calm, cool, and collected Patient, well balanced Consistent life Quiet, but witty Sympathetic and kind Keeps emotions hidden Happily reconciled to life All-purpose person
W O R K	Volunteers for jobs Thinks up new activities Looks great on the surface Creative and colorful Has energy and enthusiasm Starts in a flashy way Inspires others to join Charms others to work	Goal oriented Sees the whole picture Organizes well Seeks practical solutions Moves quickly to action Delegates work Insists on production Makes the goal Stimulates activity Thrives on opposition	Schedule oriented Perfectionist, high standards Detail conscious Persistent and thorough Orderly and organized Neat and tidy Economical Sees the problems Finds creative solutions Needs to finish what he starts Likes charts, graphs, figures, lists	Competent and steady Peaceful and agreeable Has administrative abIlity Mediates problems Avoids conflicts Good under pressure Finds the easy way
F R I E N D S	Makes friends easily Loves people Thrives on compliments Seems exciting Envied by others Doesn't hold grudges Apologizes quickly Prevents dull moments Likes spontaneous activities	Has little need for friends Will work for group activity Will lead and organize Is usually right Excels in emergencies	Makes friends cautiously Content to stay in background Avoids causing attention Faithful and devoted Will listen to complaints Can solve other's problems Deep concern for other people Moved to tears with compassion Seeks ideal mate	Easy to get along with Pleasant and enjoyable Inoffensive Good listener Dry sense of humor Enjoys watching people Has many friends Has compassion and concern

WEAKNESSES

	SANGUINE-POPULAR	CHOLERIC-POWERFUL	MELANCHOLY-PERFECT	PHLEGMATIC-PEACEFUL
E M O T I O N S	Compulsive talker Exaggerates and elaborates Dwells on trivia Can't remember names Scares others off Too happy for some Has restless energy Egotistical Blusters and complains Naive, gets taken in Has loud voice and laugh Controlled by circumstances Gets angry easily Seems phony to some Never grows up	Bossy Impatient Quick-tempered Can't relax Too impetuous Enjoys controversy and argu- ments Won't give up when losing Comes on too strong Inflexible Is not complimentary Dislikes tears and emotions Is unsympathetic	Remembers the negatives Moody and depressed Enjoys being hurt Has false humility Off in another world Low self-image Has selective hearing Self-centered Too introspective Guilt feelings Persecution complex Tends to hypochondria	Unenthusiastic Fearful and worried Indecisive Avoids responsibility Quiet will of iron Selfish Too shy and reticent Too compromising Self-righteous
W O R K	Would rather talk Forgets obligations Doesn't follow through Confidence fades fast Undisciplined Priorities out of order Decides by feelings Easily distracted Wastes time talking	Little tolerance for mistakes Doesn't analyze details Bored by trivia May make rash decisions May be rude or tactless Manipulates people Demanding of others End justifies the means Work may become his god Demands loyalty in the ranks	Not people oriented Depressed over imperfections Chooses difficult work Hesitant to start projects Spends too much time planning Prefers analysis to work Self-deprecating Hard to please Standards often too high Deep need for approval	Not goal oriented Lacks self-motivation Hard to get moving Resents being pushed Lazy and careless Discourages others Would rather watch
F R I E N D S	Hates to be alone Needs to be center stage Wants to be popular Looks for credit Dominates conversations Interrupts and doesn't listen Answers for others Fickle and forgetful Makes excuses Repeats stories	Tends to use people Dominates others Decides for others Knows everything Can do everything better Is too independent Possessive of friends and mate Can't say, "I'm sorry" May be right, but unpopular	Lives through others Insecure socially Withdrawn and remote Critical of others Holds back affection Dislikes those in opposition Suspicious of people Antagonistic and vengeful Unforgiving Full of contradictions Skeptical of compliments	Dampens enthusiasm Stays uninvolved Is not exciting Indifferent to plans Judges others Sarcastic and teasing Resists change

Living Out Love

A Journal

Dear Lori,

What I'm about to share with you is something no one else in the world knows about or has seen. I began keeping a journal the day Mark was born. At the time, I was filled with questions and wonder and thanksgiving about becoming a mother, and there seemed to be no real outlet for my feelings. I felt overwhelmed with a longing to better understand my new role as Mark's mother—as well as the roles of daughter, wife, and daughter-in-law which I'd been growing into for years. Putting my feelings and prayers into words helped me sort them out at the time, and over the years my journal has provided me with a perspective on the many ways I've changed and matured.

It seems we're never finished learning. As a new grandmother (and a relatively new mother-in-law) I'm still marveling at the way God presents us with fresh opportunities to learn His lessons and to draw nearer to Him as we do. Perhaps you're feeling challenged in the same way by your new roles of mother and daughter-in-law and wondering how others have worked them out. I offer these pages of my life not as an example of the "right" way to face such challenges, but to give you a glimpse of a side of myself that you otherwise could never know.

Because I didn't write in my journal every day, and because I'm sharing with you only the pages most relevant to our relationship, it may be difficult for you to tell how long I struggled to find answers to the questions and problems addressed here. Many of them have taken a lifetime to work out. Some remain unsolved. But regardless of the outcome, each challenge has allowed me to pursue excellence and discipline in my relationship to God and to those I love. I pray the same for you.

I love you and thank you—not only for my precious grandson, but for the happiness you bring to Joel and me, and to our son.

Your mother-in-law and friend,
Mary Beth

January 12

"Mary Beth, it's a boy!" I'll never forget those words, or the moment when the doctor held him up and I could see that I'd delivered a healthy baby boy. I was so tired! I looked back at Joel (a new dad!) and he had tears in his eyes. My legs were shaking, and our brand new baby, Mark, was wailing. The room was filled with an incredible mixture of emotions—joy, fear, love, tenderness, peace. It's a memory that will always have a special place in my heart. Instantly I whispered a prayer of thanks, and a prayer that I would do a good job of mothering this little boy. Bringing a son into the world has made me feel close to God as creator and life-giver. What a miracle our baby is!

By evening the word had spread to friends and relatives about Mark's safe arrival. Six hundred miles was too far for Mom and Dad to drive on a moment's notice. (None of us expected a first baby to be two weeks early!) I wish they lived closer. Since Joel's parents live across town, they came to the hospital right away for a visit and a peek at their new grandson. It wasn't the same as having my own mom and dad there, but I'm glad they came. They even brought a celebratory bottle of champagne. It was a little awkward when everyone but me wanted to "toast the new member of the family." Connie's always had trouble accepting the fact that I don't drink. (And I have a problem with the fact that they drink so much!) I wasn't in any mood for controversy, though, so I let them pour me a glass and kept *my feelings to myself. Thank goodness there was a NO SMOKING sign posted in the hospital room. I'd have had to put up with their cigarette smoke, too! I hate this feeling of over-protectiveness, but becoming a mother seems to have made me even more concerned about people's habits. I know Connie and Carl have the potential to influence Mark as his grandparents, and I so want that influence to be a positive one. Something I can't control, I know. Thank you, God, for my precious baby son!*

January 13

I remember reading about new mothers having "the blues." I really felt them last night in the hospital. For nine months my baby and I were inseparable—and suddenly we were spending the night in different rooms. It occurred to me that giving birth was really the first step a mother takes in letting go of her child. It's hard not to be afraid of the challenge that lies ahead for Joel and me. Dear God, help me to see this baby as Your child, in our care.

January 23

Since I came home from the hospital, Connie's called or stopped by several times a week with a casserole or groceries or some cleaning she picked up for me. It's handy having them live nearby. She's really trying to be useful and supportive in practical ways. Actually, this is the first time I can remember asking for her help. I've always done things for myself, I guess, and it was hard to change and ask

Connie for a hand. Maybe this will make a difference in our relationship. Lots of times, when Connie irritated or upset me, I've resented the fact that I "inherited" her along with Joel. I never stopped to think that she "inherited" me too. Taking care of Mark has made me look at the bond between a mother and child a little differently and has given me a new perspective on Connie—how much she loves her son, and how connected to him she must feel as his mom, even though he's grown.

How will Mark look as a grown man, I wonder? Who will he marry? Will he choose someone like me?

January 25

Connie just left after a long lunch visit. She got caught up in telling war stories about delivering Joel years ago! At first I was bothered—it seemed she was trying to turn the spotlight on herself. But then it occurred to me that maybe she didn't mean to sound so bossy and superior. Maybe that was just her way of trying to connect with me. We've never seemed to be able to find common interests, and our friendship has never been a close one. I've always thought we'd have gotten along better if she'd had a daughter, along with her three boys. But now we have childbirth in common, and we both have sons. Before she left, she leaned over and gave me a brief hug. "Thank you for giving us such a beautiful, healthy grandson," she said. I was touched. "You're welcome," I said. "I'm glad he has a grandma to love him so well."

Joel and I did some goal-setting on New Year's Eve, a few weeks before Mark was born. I hope it'll become a tradition for our family. Setting goals seemed more practical than making resolutions, which I've always had a hard time keeping. I told him that one of my priorities for this year was to really work on my relationship with Connie, especially in the disciplines of patience and acceptance. If anyone realizes the challenge of this goal, it's her oldest son! But Joel seemed sincerely pleased that I wanted to improve my relationship with his mom and promised to hold me accountable through the year. I believe that change is possible, with God's help and my commitment. It's not easy. And I know it won't come right away. But it's possible.

April 9
Sometimes it almost frightens me to think how much I love this little boy. What a phenomenon that his life began as a cell the size of a grain of sand—especially now, when I look at his grabbing hands and squirming body. I'm already starting to see glimpses of Joel and myself in Mark's features and personality. He's got his dad's funny little yawn and big ears, but his blonde hair and flirting eyes are definitely mine. I expect he'll win a few hearts when he's older!

It's too soon to know what kind of a personality our son will have. I'd love it if he were easygoing and funny, like his dad. Some of my friends have told me that one of the hardest things about parenting is accepting your child's temperament, especially if it's different from your own. Things like manners, respect, and obedience can be taught and modeled, but other things—like an outgoing personality or creativity—are apparently there when babies are born. Like the color of his eyes or the size of his feet! I hope that Joel and I can remember, as Mark grows up, that our task isn't to "make him" into a certain kind of person but to accept him as our son, to help him discover and become the person he was created to be.

April 18

As I thought more about the difficulties Connie and I have had, I came face to face with some of my own shortcomings as a daughter-in-law. I realize that many of the "character flaws" I've resented in her are just a result of her disposition, which is so different from mine! I worry about things a lot, and I can be very stubborn. Sometimes I'm so anxious to avoid conflict that I just bottle my feelings up inside myself. And I find disagreements and change very difficult.

Connie and I have hurt each other's feelings often because we're so different. She comes on so strong that it's hard for me to feel understood. She's seldom complimentary, no matter how hard I try to please her, and she seems very unsympathetic and uncomfortable with my tears and shows of emotion when I feel criticized or unappreciated. I'd like to be able to accept her just as she is, without judging *her temperament as "bad" or "wrong," just because she's more practical than I am. I'm praying that God will give me the grace to love and accept all different kinds of people and, especially, that I'll begin to relate to my mother-in-law with more patience and understanding.*

April 30

Yesterday I had a chance to practice my new approach with Connie! I was complaining about being tired after getting up with Mark for a two o'clock feeding. (I know she bottle-fed Joel and her other two boys, and she seems to think breast-feeding is repulsive in some way. She always leaves the room if I need to nurse Mark while she's there.) Anyway, she told me in an impatient voice that I should be bottle-feeding Mark. Joel could help out with the feedings, she said, and I wouldn't be so tired all the time. Besides that, she went on, I had no way of knowing how much the baby was getting to eat, the way I would if he were drinking from a bottle. She sounded like such an expert that, for a second, I was at a loss for words. Before long, I regained my determination. Hurtful retaliations were on the tip of my tongue. But just before I spoke, I remembered the goal I set in January—to be patient with Connie and considerate of her feelings.

"I understand that you're not really comfortable around me when I'm nursing Mark. I know you didn't breast-feed your children, and you must have had some good reasons for choosing the bottle. But to tell you the truth, I

feel good about breast-feeding. I like the way my body provides food for him, and I feel a wonderful bond when I'm able to hold him close and nourish him. It's almost as though he were still a part of me." I held my breath…but she seemed to be waiting for me to go on!

"I know I've complained about being tired. I'm probably not napping when I should and maybe I'm trying to do too much around the house. I'm sorry if I've been a grump. My body's probably still adjusting to having given birth and all the extra work. But Joel and I agree that breast-feeding is the best choice for Mark. If you're uncomfortable being in the room, I can find somewhere else to sit—or it's fine for you to leave until we're finished."

Connie couldn't think of a thing to say. I think she was surprised by such a direct approach from someone who usually just sat back and "took it"! What a difference the words "I understand" and "I'm sorry" seemed to make! Maybe Connie appreciated the fact that I was sensitive to her misgivings but that I was sure enough about my decision to stick with it. It was a small victory, but a victory all the same. Thank you, God!

August 19
Diane has always been a great neighbor, but these last eighteen months, since Mark burst onto the scene, she's really helped me understand the meaning of the word "friend." She's a woman of deep concern and sensitivity.

More than once she's brought over a spaghetti dinner or a pot of soup at the end of an especially hectic day or offered to watch the baby while I did errands for a few hours in the afternoon. And her meals are works of art! She's so creative in the kitchen. The food is not only delicious but elegant, too. She even makes motherhood look easy. Today I felt a little envious when we had lunch at her house. Diane's so organized and proficient, with everything in its place. Even little Carolyn's room looks like a page from a catalog, with the perfectly made canopy bed and the dolls all lined up on the window seat. (I'll bet Connie hoped her son would bring home someone like Diane instead of me—they'd have hit it off just great.) I wished I'd paid attention to Mark's clothes this morning. He doesn't look picture perfect very often these days, and neither do I. Diane always seems so polished and put together. I wonder if she looked this good when Carolyn was almost two!

While we were eating lunch, I noticed a list on the refrigerator with the meals for the week all written out. I can't imagine being that organized and methodical. When I asked her if she made a list every week, she acted surprised at the question. It made shopping more efficient, she explained, and she didn't have to think about what to cook each night. How do I know on Monday what I'm going to want for dinner on Friday? I guess I'm more like my Mom!

Still, it's fun to have a friend who's different from me and yet accepts me just as I am. Diane has high standards, but she's not critical. At first she was a little reluctant to commit to walking with me every other morning, but once we got started, she admitted how much she's enjoying it. I am, too. It's good exercise, and it's given us some time to visit. I'm thankful for her friendship and all I'm learning about myself as a result of it.

October 8

Well, yesterday Connie brought over a little devil costume for Mark to wear this Halloween. It's in a few weeks, and she told me how much fun Joel and his brothers had dressing up each year. I didn't know what to say! We never celebrated Halloween at our house. I don't think I ever even had a costume (although I remember feeling left out when everyone else was talking about theirs). What to do…I hate to disappoint Connie, but I don't think I want Mark dressing up like the devil, this year or any year! I wonder how Joel feels about it…

October 15

This morning, as we were walking past neighborhood houses decorated with grave markers and skeletons, Diane asked me if Joel and Mark and I would like to trick-or-treat around the block with Carolyn. I told her we'd never celebrated Halloween, and that Connie had given Mark a little devil costume to wear. I wasn't sure how to handle it. I just hate this holiday!

*She just laughed. "We don't 'celebrate' Halloween either,"
she said. "But Carolyn likes the dress-up part, and I
always did, too. It was fun and harmless. What's wrong
with that?"*

*I gave her the same explanation my parents always gave
me, that Halloween is based on some pagan rituals and
beliefs that conflicted with what we believe. To me that
makes sense. The Bible is clear about staying away from
anything having to do with demons and witches, fortune
telling, Ouija boards, and the occult. It seemed to me that
these are all the things Halloween's about. Dressing Mark
up as the devil and going trick-or-treating would just be
taking part in something that's against what I believe.*

*Diane seemed to understand that but reminded me that
declaring a taboo on Halloween would be difficult as he
gets older. I told her our church has a harvest party on the
31st of October, with candy and family games. I hoped he'd
make some good friends in the church and that they'd feel
the same way. I felt a little awkward being so outspoken
about Halloween, but it gave me a concrete way to define
the context of my faith and its Christian basis. I was tempt-
ed to ask Diane about her church background and beliefs,
but the timing didn't seem right. At least we'd broken the ice!*

October 11
*The next time we walked, Diane asked me what I
planned to do about the outfit Connie sent. I told her I*

wasn't sure. Connie isn't easily discouraged and comes across as if she knows what's right and best for everyone. Usually I don't make much of our differences, but in this case I felt it was important to let her know we had different feelings about Halloween. I was considering returning the costume to her and inviting her to choose something else for Mark to "dress-up" in when he and his friends pretend, maybe a fireman's hat or some cowboy boots. Diane thought that would be a gracious solution.

"Be glad your mother-in-law shows interest in Mark," she said, "even if you don't always agree. I never hear from Steven's mother. Carolyn's her only grandchild, and you'd think she'd be the doting grandmother. But she has her priorities all out of order. She's late with birthday presents and just sends a check at Christmas. Finally, I said something to her about being so distracted and forgetful when it came to Carolyn. Mrs. Fleming got so angry at me that we haven't spoken since."

This was the first time Diane had mentioned her mother-in-law, and I could tell she was devastated by the break-down in their relationship. Just calling her "Mrs. Fleming" sounded formal and awkward. Diane's comment has given me a new outlook on my own mother-in-law. Connie and I have had our share of problems and differences, but we've always managed to work them out. Thanks, God, for this glimpse at a relationship much more troubled than the one I've been complaining about.

December 26

Well, it seems everything went wrong this Christmas. I'd hoped this year would be our best ever—Connie and I had been getting along much better lately. But nothing about the holidays went smoothly! For one thing, Connie and Carl had agreed to have Christmas dinner at our house this year. But at the last minute she came up with several reasons that it "just wouldn't be possible..." including the fact that her dog was not well and couldn't go in the car or be left alone! Once again, she seemed to be inflexible and needing to have more of the control she was used to during the holiday season. Joel reminded me of my goal to have a smoother relationship with his mom. So, even though I'd have preferred to stay in my own house and have the in-laws here, protesting didn't seem worth it.

But I'd forgotten how difficult it could be to be in Connie's house over the holidays. She has her own particular way of doing everything, and I couldn't seem to get anything right—I even loaded the dishwasher "wrong"! She was full of advice about Mark (he isn't eating enough vegetables, I let him drink too much milk with his meals, he sometimes forgets to say please and thank you). And she even mumbled under her breath at the church service that Joel and I were showing "too much affection in public" when he put his arm around me during the prayer! I had to exercise great restraint to keep from attacking her in return each time she came up with a criticism. It's true that her generation had different ideas about nutrition and showing affection (and they didn't even have dish-washers!) so it's not surprising that we don't agree on some things. But I did finally tell her that we were happy with the way Mark was growing and developing, and the pediatrician didn't have any concerns about his eating habits. And Joel and I continued to put our arms around one another whenever we felt like it. Maybe she and Carl can learn a thing or two from us on that one!

On Christmas Eve she asked me to season the turkey. She was busy doing other things, and I was happy to help out. But when I took out some herbs from the cabinet, she immediately stopped what she was doing and came over to correct me and show me the "right" ones to use. I let her know exactly how I was feeling!

"If you wanted this done a certain way, I wish you had told me, or done it yourself. I'm willing to help out, Connie, but I don't appreciate being criticized at every turn. I can do something differently from you without being wrong." She told me to go ahead with what I'd chosen, and the turkey turned out great. She probably found my words offensive and would never have spoken to her mother-in-law that directly, but I felt better clearing the air.

One of the toughest moments came on Christmas morning when Mark opened his Christmas gift from Connie and Carl—they'd given him a gun! She and Carl knew very well that Joel and I don't like kids using weapons as toys—especially a five-year-old—and yet they went ahead and got it for him anyway. I couldn't believe my eyes when I saw it!

"It was really Carl's idea," Connie said. "He's hoping that Mark will be joining him on the deer hunts one of these days. And it's just a little toy cap gun, Mary Beth. What can that hurt?"

What hurt most was that she'd gone against my wishes. Also, she seemed to act as though it were all right simply because she was his grandmother and we were in her house and this gave her some measure of authority over me as his mother. I was so furious I wanted to explode! But Connie and I had already had our share of disagreements, and I decided to let Joel handle his mom on this one. Mark had taken the gun out of the box and begun firing at everything in sight by the time we realized what it was. A few years ago, I might have thought she was trying to test my patience by giving Mark something she knew I didn't want him to have. But he'd told everyone that all he wanted for Christmas was a cap gun. I know she was just trying to make him happy—even if it was at my expense. He was thrilled, and Connie and Carl were clearly pleased to have given him something he liked so much. If only it could have been something besides a gun. God, you'll have to help me out here. Please give me some patience, and don't let the sun go down on my anger!

December 27

*J*oel and I decided to let Mark keep the gun. But he made it clear to his parents that, in the future, we want them to let us know ahead of time if they planned to give Mark something we might not approve of. He also told Carl that he wanted Mark to understand guns weren't toys and that it would be years before Mark was old enough to accompany his grandfather on a deer hunt.

Joel was as hurt and confused about the whole episode as I was. I was glad he and I were in agreement on the subject, and that he was able to express our feelings this time, instead of me. We want to get along with his parents, but our values are different in many ways. It's hard not to see these disagreements as an issue of "right versus wrong," especially since we were brought up to "respect our elders" and "do as we're told." But since Joel and I became parents ourselves, we're now in a position of authority over Mark. Is the hierarchy of submission more complicated these days? Or have relationships always been this demanding? My prayer today is for more diplomacy in my communication with those who see things differently from me.

December 28

*C*onnie said something as we walked to the car today which gave me a little bit of hope. We were taking our gifts out to the car, and their German shepherd, Nicky, was barking at the neighbor's cat. Connie's never been too fond *of him, and now I know why. "Carl's mother gave Joel that dog for his birthday when he was a teenager, as a surprise," she said, and she frowned, remembering it. "We were all surprised. No one had asked my permission. I had a house full of teenage boys, and I certainly didn't want to have to look out for a puppy!" I could hear in her voice the anger she'd felt after her own mother-in-law made such a big decision without consulting her. She didn't mention the cap gun again—not even an apology! But maybe this memory will help her understand my frustration. I hope so.*

The last thing I wanted was for our visit to end on a sour note. I said the only gracious thing I could think of. "I know it was a lot of extra work to have us here for so much of the Christmas holiday, Connie, and I appreciate all you did. I hope you can see that I'm doing the best I can to be a good mom to Mark and a good wife to Joel. It's important to me that you know that. And about the gun—it means a lot to me that you want to give Mark the things he's asked for, even if we don't always agree about them. I know how much you love him." Connie didn't apologize or even assure me that things between us were fine (she never does) but at least I was able to leave knowing I'd done my part toward more understanding— and honesty—in our relationship.

February 12

A͟s we were walking this morning, Diane told me that Steven had asked her whether she thought a reconciliation between her and his mother was possible. She told me that all of the problems I'd experienced with Connie and the progress I'd made had given her some hope, and though she hadn't admitted it to Steven yet, she was willing to try. I felt like celebrating! I could tell that God was working in her heart. She asked me what she could do to break the silence and begin to mend their broken relationship.

I told her that when I'm not absolutely sure what to do, I find it helpful to pray. Sometimes God sends an answer in the form of a good idea. We prayed about Diane's desire to please Steven and to establish communication with Mrs. Fleming again, and when we were finished, Diane said, "I think I'll write her a letter. I know what I want to say." She didn't tell me what she planned to write, but I saw a peace in her face that I've never seen before. It'll be exciting to see the changes that God brings about as a result of Diane's willingness to reach out to Mrs. Fleming. Thanks for miracles, Lord, big and small!

March 14 (after our move to the northeast)
I wish I could relax a little about this weekend. Carl and Connie are coming for Mark's confirmation, and I've spent the whole week cleaning house! I don't know why I'm always afraid Connie will show up with a white glove to check for dust. In the past, she's been complimentary about my taste in decorating and my housekeeping. But since I've started teaching piano lessons in the afternoons, I have less time to spend on housework. I guess I'm still

trying to appear the perfect wife and mother in Connie's eyes. I wonder if I'll ever feel acceptable to her...

I can already tell how much more energy and effort a long distance relationship with Joel's parents will demand. When we lived in the same city, we saw them frequently, but the visits were short. We could pick up the phone whenever we needed to, without thinking about the cost. Now we only talk to them twice a month, and Connie's already started to complain about all the time we're spending with my family. Has she forgotten how many Mother's Days, Thanksgivings, and Easters we spent at her house?

A lot of the complaining takes place over the phone when Connie talks to Joel. I don't hear about it until after the conversation has ended, and he feels caught in the middle, trying to please both his mother and his wife. Total frustration for all of us!

Part of that is my fault, I guess. When Connie calls, I just say hello and then hand the phone to Joel. Maybe she'd tell me some of these things herself if I gave her more of a chance. She's actually a better communicator through letters than she is on the phone. She's so quick-tempered that she says things without thinking, and her words can really sting. But her letters are usually thoughtful and well-stated. After one of their visits north, she wrote: "Thank you for the time we spent with you and Mark. The visit passed ever so quickly. He is a credit to his Mom and Dad."

I'll never forget those words. It's one of the nicest compliments she's ever given me. It's amazing how soothing words can be, and how helpful it is to be able to go back and read a kind letter when I need a lift. I even feel I've gotten to know her better, in some ways, now that we live so far apart and have to depend on writing things down to keep in touch. During this visit, I'm going to make a real effort at being more vulnerable with Connie. I know there are things I can learn from her if only I'm not too proud to listen and be teachable.

March 16

Joel and I are so happy about Mark's desire to be confirmed and the way he's growing spiritually. Connie seemed a little reluctant at first when we invited the two of them to be here for the ceremony. I don't know why— maybe she's still upset over our move to the Northeast. Or it could be our decision to transfer from "their" Presbyterian faith to an independent church. She seemed surprised to learn that our church didn't belong to any particular denomination. I'm praying that I'll be able to put my anxieties about Connie aside—at least for the weekend—and focus instead on what confirmation is all about. This could be the perfect opportunity for Connie to witness firsthand the truths about Christ that are so meaningful to Joel and to me. I'd love to have an opportunity to talk to her about her faith. Maybe God will give us that chance…

March 19

Connie and I spent an afternoon shopping before she and Carl headed back. There was a gourmet cooking store she wanted to see, and I was surprised to find how much she knew about copper cookware, electric juicers, steamers— even woks! I'd been considering getting one, and she was able to tell me everything I needed to know. Since Carl was put on a restricted diet, Connie's been experimenting with new cooking techniques and she's even begun subscribing to a gourmet cooking magazine. It was fun to discover a common interest and be able to learn something from her without feeling I was being "told" or "corrected." She seemed to enjoy the day, too, and ended up buying me the wok as a gift. I remember reading in the book of James that every good gift comes from heaven (even woks!). I know for sure that God was behind this one.

March 22

Diane called last night. I've really missed our morning walks—it's just not the same, having to catch up and solve problems long distance. She received a letter from Mrs. Fleming yesterday, and she read it to me over the phone. I could tell that it wasn't what she'd hoped for, but I told her how encouraged I was that Mrs. Fleming had written at all, and I hoped she'd persevere. It wasn't a letter of friendship but of bitterness and pain, making excuses, blaming Diane for the breakdown in communication and reciting incidents from their past which served no purpose other than to remind Diane of the reasons she'd grown so angry with Mrs. Fleming in the first place. I had to admit that if Connie had written me such a letter, it would've been a setback. But I've learned to "never say never" where God's promises are concerned. He promises to heal and to mend. He promises to comfort and console, and to forgive us as we forgive others. I prayed for Mrs. Fleming and for the healing of their relationship, in God's time. Diane was crying during our conversation. I wish I could have been there to put my arms around her. But truthfully, I knew the love and acceptance she truly desired couldn't come from her mother-in-law or from me, but only from God. Perhaps He'll use the pain of this relationship to show her this wonderful, mysterious truth.

September 2

These girls are relentless! I've always known Mark would be a heartthrob, but the eleventh grade girls are going overboard. What ever happened to the good old days when the boy was the pursuer? Thank goodness I have a while before Mark will be thinking of getting married! I've always heard of possessive mothers…now I have to fight to keep from becoming one. I guess it wouldn't hurt for me to begin praying for the ability to love Mark with more freedom—and for that lucky woman who will someday be his wife.

It seems that the day Mark began his junior year in high school was the day he really started pulling away from Joel *and me. He even rode to school that morning with a senior friend instead of going with his dad. I know Joel was disappointed not to have that time together, but he's not as emotional about Mark's getting older as I am. Guess that comes from being a mom…*

I remember my junior year in high school and the way Mother always tried to pal around with my friends and me. It drove me crazy! Teenagers just don't like being with their parents the way they did when they were small. It's hard, because I still think of Mark as my little boy. I remember when he was six or seven and he would come home from school full of news and little drawings to show me. In the afternoons, we'd go to the library or over to the Y, where he might have a ball game. He always wanted me to stay and watch him practice. I still have as much interest in him and his friends and activities as I ever did. It's just that he's growing up, and I know he's looking to others now—as well as to me—for support and encouragement.

There have been so many times in the past when I've resented Connie for treating Joel as if he were still a twelve-year-old. I'm starting to understand that, because she's his mother, she'll always feel some kind of responsibility for him, the way I do for Mark. It must be harder and harder to give that up as boys grow older and more independent. But I'm sure Mark doesn't want a controlling mother any more than I want a controlling mother-in-law! This has even been an issue for Joel, at times. It's been hard for me to see him at odds with Connie over her "meddling." But at least I know I'm not the only one she wants to "help"! She sent him a package after her last visit—a dozen pairs of boxer shorts! She said she'd noticed how worn his had become and thought he needed some new ones. I thought it was kind of funny, and something only a mother would do, but Joel phoned her right away and said he would be sending them back. He liked his shorts "broken in" and didn't need any new ones. I guess men struggle sometimes with feeling caught between being a son and being a husband, the same way I've felt pulled between being a daughter and being a wife and mother. Sometimes I just want someone to take care of me for a change, and it's nice to pay my mom a visit and be pampered.

At least Connie adores Mark. I'm really thankful for that, particularly after hearing Diane talk of Carolyn's sadness not to really know or see her grandmother. In fact, Connie's love for her son and grandson is one of the few things that really binds us together these days. It's hard being the parent of a teenager. Mark's at an impressionable age, and I've appreciated the notes of encouragement that she's sent him about his tennis awards and his progress toward earning Eagle Scout. (If only she didn't send him money along with the notes! She and Carl think everything good in life deserves to be recognized in dollars and cents. Just another way we're different, I guess.) She told me she's been working on a scrapbook of his accomplishments to give to him at graduation next spring. What a neat surprise that'll be for him. I remember how overwhelmed I was as a new bride to receive a handmade cookbook of family recipes that she'd put together and an address book filled with names, addresses, and birthdays of all the relatives. At first I was intimidated by so much information—what if my meals didn't turn out exactly the same? What if I forgot to send a birthday card after she'd gone to the trouble of writing all of the dates down? I was so worried about disappointing Connie that I saw her gifts as challenges rather than the helpful gestures they were intended to be. I have to laugh at myself when I realize how much I've grown and changed over the years. Since we moved away, Connie has seemed to develop more of a balance between her commitment to us and the time she spends with her friends and taking care of Carl. I know Joel wishes he could be there to help her more, now that Carl's cancer has progressed. Caring for him is taking a lot out of her. But, in a way, the distance has helped relationships between all of us. Living in the same town put a great strain on us at times. I think we all felt an obligation to spend more time together than we sometimes wanted to. Now, visits and phone calls are things we all look forward to, especially since Carl's situation has worsened. Time is precious. I realize this more every day...

June 8

Carl died. Connie phoned from the emergency room around midnight with the news. Mark and Joel and I will be flying to be with her this afternoon, but I just had to get my thoughts down. His lung cancer has been a long and painful trial for them both. Joel said he couldn't help but feel relief as well as sadness when she said that he'd finally died. I understood because I felt the same way. Carl seemed to know the time was near. He was a Christian of deep faith, and Connie said he'd asked her to read to him from the Psalms early last evening, before his lungs began to fail. I know that gave both of them peace.

I think Mark had been mentally preparing for Carl's death for some time. When Joel broke the news to him this morning, he was sad but not surprised. This is his first real experience with death. I was just a little younger than he is when my grandfather died. He wanted to go with us and be with Connie, and also to attend the memorial service. Mark came up and put his arms around me as I packed our suitcases. Though I was relieved for Carl to be free from suffering now, I think Mark sensed my grief. "He's in heaven now, Mom…" Mark said. It was as though he was consoling us both, reminding us that one of God's most perfect promises had finally been fulfilled for Carl.

Joel is such a private person that I let him know I shared his sorrow but was willing to wait until he was ready to talk about it. One thing he said impressed me deeply. "I loved my dad as much as a son could," he said. "It's hard to believe he's gone. But I feel closer to him, in a way, knowing that he's with our Father in heaven, and that he's finally well."

I've often wondered about Connie's commitment to Christ. She and I have never been able to talk comfortably about our beliefs. I know that God is using each of us in Connie's life as He sees fit. Surely Carl was a witness to the love of Christ throughout their marriage. And Joel is such a fine and godly man. Even Mark has been able to talk to Connie about some spiritual matters that she and I have never discussed. My prayer is that she'll feel God's love and comfort more than ever, now that she's alone, and that my faith will be a testimony to her through the things I do and say.

I didn't realize it before, but I've never seen Connie cry. She's a woman of great strength in many ways, and tears make us so vulnerable. More and more, as Connie reveals her humanity to me, I feel myself wanting to connect with her and believing it's possible for us to grow closer.

June 12
A long week of family grieving is over. As I packed to fly back home, I was so glad that Rob and his family live near Connie. She'll welcome their help and company once things settle down.

Joel talked privately with Ted and Rob before we left about Connie's living alone—what to do with the house, whether a smaller place might be more sensible, and whether, over the long term, any of the brothers would consider having her move in. I understood the concern about the house, but the discussion about Connie living with one of her sons seemed premature—maybe because I don't feel prepared to face that possibility of change in our life. Joel said they agreed that as long as Connie's health remained good and she was able to take care of herself, he didn't see any reason to sell the house. Rob and Jean and the children have been spending a lot of time over there during Carl's illness, and I know that their visits will be even more frequent now. The house and yard accommodate everyone so much better than an apartment or condo would.

Joel said he felt a little guilty that Rob will be shouldering so much of the responsibility for looking after Connie. With Ted on the West Coast and our living so far north, we won't be able to help as much as either of us would like.

But Rob wisely pointed out that there's a season for everything. This is the time when he and Jean can be of help to Connie. Later on, perhaps in a few years, it'll be Ted's and Joel's turns, in whatever ways are necessary. In the meantime, I'd like to think of some ways I can serve her from a distance. Maybe I can begin writing to her regularly. I've been very sporadic about keeping in touch, and I know that mail will become more important to her, now that she's living alone.

I'm thankful that Joel and his brothers have a close relationship and care so much for their mom and for each other. Aging and loss are never easy, but they're inevitable. Sharing the burden makes all difficult phases more tolerable—and I can feel the family unity as everyone works toward a common goal: protecting and providing for Connie.

September 25

It seems like a long time since I wrote in this journal. With Mark away at college, things are much less busy around here. Joel enrolled in an evening computer course at the community college, and it's taken more of his time than either of us expected. He hasn't said so, but I sense that he's having some of the same empty nest feelings that I'm experiencing. Our relationship and its focus are changing now that Mark's away from home. It's not that I didn't anticipate the change—I'm just having difficulty adjusting to it.

Connie phoned the other day, and it was as if she sensed some of what we are going through. She mentioned how difficult it had been to get used to Joel's room being empty once he left for college and asked if we were doing all right. Connie hasn't been known for her timing nor her tact, so I was moved by her attempt to reach out to me when she's still adjusting to the dramatic loss in her own life.

I told her that her phone call was just what the doctor ordered. "It's been a real adjustment for us," I said, "but I'm beginning to see a light at the end of the tunnel. Besides, Mark is planning to come home for Thanksgiving—only seven more weeks!" We laughed and moved on to other family matters—some investments Joel was handling for her, and a trip we were planning to take to visit her soon. God is so gracious in His timing. I pray I'll always remember that when I feel He has asked me to handle something before I feel really prepared, He knows best what I'm able to bear.

November 4
Diane surprised me with a phone call this morning. Steven's parents had written asking her and Steven to join the two of them for Thanksgiving. Diane is considering the possibility, but the last time they spent a holiday together things didn't go well. I admire her persistence in this relationship, particularly under the circumstances. Mrs. Fleming sounds like a very troubled woman—she's so easily angered, exaggerating wrongs and dwelling on past hurts. Diane feels such a deep need for approval from her, and it seems she may never get it. "Steven really wants to go," Diane said. "His dad isn't well, and although neither of them has made the effort to visit Steven, they expect him to show up when they invite him. But I just don't know if I'm ready to face her again. Carolyn was hoping we could fly up and spend Thanksgiving with her, in Georgetown." I could tell that Georgetown was where

Diane really wanted to be—with her daughter, where she knew she was loved.

"How would it feel if Steven were to go to his parents' house this year and you were to spend Thanksgiving weekend with Carolyn in Georgetown—you two could have lots of time together, enjoy a meal somewhere, shop, whatever you want. Steven could visit with his mom and dad."

"It sounds ideal," Diane said. "If only that were possible."

I told her that it was possible. Just because Steven had never visited his parents without her didn't mean it wasn't possible, or even desirable. It provided a way for everyone, including Carolyn, to be where they wanted to be at Thanksgiving. "Who knows," I said. "Maybe Mrs. Fleming would even enjoy having Steven to herself…"

"Maybe she would," Diane sighed. "But she's so unreasonable. She only sees part of the picture. For instance, she wouldn't take Carolyn's wishes into consideration, or my own mixed feelings about our relationship. She'd just see that she'd invited Steven and me, and only Steven came. She'd find that rude and unforgivable."

I knew Diane was in a difficult position because I'd been there myself. The first time Joel went to visit his parents without me was just a few years ago, and it had taken me months to feel comfortable with my decision to stay home.

But it was the right decision for everyone. Connie and I had had enough of each other for a while, and Joel said that she was able to relax and really enjoy his company in a way that didn't seem possible when I was around. I don't know why we didn't consider it years ago. Joel enjoyed visiting his parents frequently, but there were many times when Connie and I certainly could have benefited from a brief separation.

"It worked for us," I told Diane. "Don't rule out the possibility. Even if Mrs. Fleming doesn't understand right away, you'll know that you've done the best you could in working out a difficult situation." I pray that God will give her the wisdom to do what is best for everyone involved—not just her mother-in-law, whom she wants so desperately to please.

March 22

Connie hasn't really been the same person since Carl died. Seeing her cope with making decisions which used to be Carl's responsibilities—like buying a new car—have made me aware of how much I rely on Joel in our marriage. I'm considering signing up for a course about financial planning in retirement years. I'd like to understand more about the stock market and our own investments, particularly since I'm so much younger than Joel. I can hardly face the thought of outliving him, but I know the odds are that I will.

I have a new respect for Connie as I watch her begin to make a life for herself alone. She seems less "Joel's mother" or "my mother-in-law" to me lately, and more just "Connie." I wish I'd been able to see her as an individual early in our marriage, the way I do now. I think there would have been less jealousy and resentment between us. Maybe that's something that only comes with maturity. I wonder if Connie is able to see me as an individual too, and not just as "Joel's wife."

Now that he's asked me to think about her coming to live with us, I'm especially glad that she and I have overcome some of the barriers that used to keep us from having a good relationship. It's difficult to imagine all the changes that having her in our home full-time would bring. I wonder about where she'd sleep. I guess I'd have to let her take the sewing room. Or she could take Mark's room, but I feel like he needs a place of his own when he comes home. I wonder what it would be like if Joel and I were going away for the weekend to leave her here alone. He and I have started traveling more since Mark has been in college. Lots to think about. I know how important it is to Joel that his mom feels welcome and be well provided for in her later years. And as I pray about the decision, I keep reminding myself that caring for Connie, whatever her needs may become, is one way I can show my love for him.

October 18

Joel and I just returned from a fun Parents' Weekend with Mark. Connie joined us, at Mark's request. I have to admit that I was feeling selfish at first and wished Joel and I could have Mark to ourselves. But he was showing a remarkable sensitivity, I think, in including her and, as it turned out, we all had a wonderful visit. I'm especially thankful for their good relationship after knowing first-hand about grandparents like the Flemings who pay no attention to their grandchildren. What a world of joy they're missing.

Saturday night we went out to dinner, and Connie and Mark spent some time reminiscing about a trip she and Carl took with Mark across Canada one summer. I realized for the first time that he'll always see Connie differently than I do—he hasn't had to prove himself to her, or experience her possessive, demanding side. To her, Mark can do no wrong. To him, she's just "Grandma," and she's deeply loved.

January 10

I'm thankful that Mom and Dad are so healthy and have such a good marriage. With all of this transition going on, I don't think I could manage one more set of responsibilities! Mark has gradually broken away from Joel and me and will probably be settling down before too long. At the same time, Connie has lost her lifetime partner and is needing more care and attention than we're used to giving her. Relationships can really be tough when the roles keep changing.

I've always loved the idea of Christ being the same, yesterday, today, and forever. I've sensed an ebb and flow in my faith, particularly during times of crisis, but I know it was a result of change within myself, not in Him. If Connie does come to live in our home and I'm to serve her daily, I'll have to rely more and more on Him to be my strength. This is one task I won't be able to do on my own!

May 19

It's hard to believe that this afternoon Mark crossed a stage to accept his college diploma. I just don't know where all the years went. I looked over at Joel to take his hand, and I still saw the same young man I fell in love with. I wonder if he still sees a young girl in me. Mark seemed so grown up in his cap and gown. He's worked hard these four years toward his degree. I'm very proud of him. It's hard to believe he's the same little boy I gave birth to twenty-two years ago.

He may be getting serious about this girl he has been seeing since Christmas. We met her and liked her very much—her parents were also nice. For many years I've been praying that Mark would fall in love with someone who would be just the right match for him, one that God had truly prepared for marriage, one who loved Him and who would be able to love Mark just as he is, faults and all! I wonder whether Lori is that woman?

When I caught Connie's eye during the graduation ceremony, I saw tears in them. I know she must have been wishing Carl could have lived long enough to see his oldest grandson graduate, especially since Mark plans to be an engineer like his grandfather. I wonder whether Joel and I will live to see Mark's children graduate from college. The idea of even being a grandmother is completely foreign to me now! I guess I'll be able to ease into that gradually, as Mark decides upon a wife and they begin a life together. I'm thankful that marriage and children didn't just suddenly descend upon us, like so many other things in life seem to. God really knows the heart of a woman…how we need a great deal of time to adjust to such important changes in our lives.

November 21

It was so much fun having Lori and Mark here for Thanksgiving. They chose the occasion to tell us they have set a wedding date! I can't say I'm surprised, but I'm certainly happy for them both, and even excited at the prospect of becoming a "mother-in-law," something I thought I'd dread. I told Lori that Joel and I have prayed for many years for the right woman for Mark, and that she was the answer to our prayers. It'll be a new experience to have a "daughter" in the family. We're already becoming good friends. There is so much to be thankful for this year.

Cooking the meal together was a great way for Lori and me to get better acquainted. I remember the first time I went home with Joel to meet his family. Not just Connie and Carl, but both brothers and his two uncles and aunts! Talk about overwhelming! Connie insisted that I sit idly by while she did all the cooking. I have a distinct memory of her hurrying around the kitchen, waving a knife in my direction when she addressed a question to me. No wonder I felt intimidated from the day we met! I know she was just trying to be a thoughtful hostess by offering to do all the work (or was it her decisive, take-charge temperament introducing itself?) but I'd really have felt more a part of the family if she'd let me help.

Anyway, I was happy to assign some jobs when Lori said she wanted to pitch in. She set the table and made the iced tea. She also folded the napkins in a decorative shape and showed me a way to cut oranges for a pretty garnish around the turkey. I was really impressed with her skills. When I mentioned that I've always loved to cook and have considered signing up for a Chinese cooking course, she said she'd enjoy that, too. I wish she and Mark had been able to find jobs a little closer to us. It would have been fun for Lori and me to take the class together. At least we're discovering some common interests—and she knows that just because I'm older I don't have all the answers.

As we were putting the dinner on the table, Lori asked if I'd mind her calling me by my first name. Since I've always been on a first-name basis with Connie, it seemed perfectly natural. But as I thought back to the pre-wedding days, I remembered feeling very awkward about the issue of names. I don't think I called Connie anything for a while! It was a relief to talk it over with Lori and to know that she felt comfortable bringing up the subject. I guess we won't have to address that question again until I become a grandmother and need yet another name! I'm not going to mention grandchildren for quite a while—but it'll sure be fun to have them some day.

November 22

M*ark was anxious to call his grandmother with the good news. This is the first Thanksgiving in years she hasn't been with us, but she sounded happy to be with Rob and his family. Without Carl, Connie's felt a little over-whelmed by the complications of long-distance travel. I hope she'll get over that in time. It would be wonderful if Joel and his brothers could all share in the responsibility of being sure she's well looked after.*

It's strange to think that Connie wasn't much older than I am now when Joel and I got married. Her life was filled with what seemed like very "grown-up" activities then— volunteer work, her book club, and the lifesaving class she taught at the Y. I remember feeling so young, just out of college and starting my first job. Now I'm the older one and Lori is setting up her first home. It's funny how the tables turn.

The generation gap seems to be closing a little, though. We're more active these days than Carl and Connie were at our age. Joel is still able to beat Mark at tennis! And since Lori is a runner, too, she and I are talking about entering a 10K race this coming spring. I can't help but think that each of our relationships will be better all the way around because of these things—good health, shared interests, open communication.

December 1

It's exciting to see Lori and Mark begin to plan a life together. It takes me back to the time when Joel and I were just starting out. During the holiday weekend, Lori looked at Mark as though he could do no wrong. I'm sure he feels the same way about her. It won't take long for her to discover that I didn't raise a perfect son. They're in for some surprises! The ironing-out process of getting to really know your partner can be rough.

I guess everyone remembers their first year of marriage, but I especially remember our 19th anniversary. I thought at the time: this is a milestone. I've now lived longer with Joel than his mother did! Even though a mom knows her son better than anyone while he's growing up, no one knows him better as an adult than his wife. This is some-thing I'm going to hide in my heart and remember as Lori and Mark start their life together. She's his partner and companion from now on. I want to be an encouragement to them both.

August 4

*H*aving Connie living with us in our home has required a tremendous amount of patience and humility, as I knew it would. Her health continues to deteriorate from her smoking—and she hasn't wanted to quit, even though the doctor has had to prescribe oxygen for her emphysema. Putting up with the smoke and the smell of cigarettes throughout our home has been a real adjustment. As her physical dependence on Joel and me has increased, her controlling personality seems to have increased, too. I know it must be hard for her to have lost the privacy and self-sufficiency she enjoyed all those years with Carl. But it's a real challenge to maintain peace in our home! She asks me to do things one way ("Could we have fish tonight, Mary Beth?") and Joel wants them another way ("You know I don't really like fish, Mary Beth. Why are you fixing it so often?"). He doesn't understand how often things like this happen. It's not so much trouble to fix Connie something special once in a while, or even to change our routine, but lately I've felt there were too many chiefs in this family! I'm praying every day for more understanding and patience with Connie. Maybe growing old is like becoming a mother—you never really know what it's like until it happens to you.

September 18

"Mom—it's a boy!" The minute Mark came out of the delivery room with the news of David's arrival, I felt transported back in time to the day Mark was born and I heard those words myself. Now my own son is a father, and Lori has become a mother—and I'm a grandmother! It's a miracle to see the cycle of life continue in my own family. New roles and responsibilities for everyone…I pray we'll handle them well.

When Mark was little, I remember feeling overwhelmed by all that was expected of me and wondering how all the other mothers managed to make it look so easy. I knew that raising children was something women had been doing for centuries. But at the same time, I believed my experience was unique and that no one had truly experienced or felt what was happening to me. Maybe I was right, at least in part—each experience is as different as each mother and child.

Lori must be feeling this confusion and sense of responsibility, too. I remember how Connie, especially at first, used to give me all kinds of advice about being a mom. Now, as I think of all that lies ahead for Lori and Mark, I can see why. I feel full of warnings and suggestions! But I don't want to come across as a know-it-all. Lori will have to figure out most of the mothering process herself, like I did. I remember how I felt when Connie chastised me for not putting a hat on Mark before going out, or giving him too much fruit with his cereal—or the time she went completely against Joel's and my wishes and gave him that toy gun. Thankfully, Lori and I started out on a more frank and friendly footing than Connie and I ever achieved. So I hope that this new phase of our lives won't present problems but will be an opportunity to experience this little baby together, each in her own way.

September 26

Having Connie live with us has had some benefits, especially for Mark. Even though he and Lori live an hour away, they have made a point of visiting every other weekend, usually on Sunday afternoon. Everyone enjoys the time together—well, there have been a few days when the atmosphere was tense, but I hope they can be forgiving and understanding of those. It's especially fun to see David and to be able to love him and care for him in person rather than through the mail and on the phone, which I have to settle for during the week.

A few weeks ago, I overheard them in Connie's bedroom looking through one of her photo albums. Mark has looked through our family albums dozens of times, but this was one Connie had been keeping over the years, and apparently he'd never seen it. One photo of Mark in his cowboy outfit prompted Connie to retell the story of the Christmas they gave him the cap gun that Joel and I didn't want him to have. And the cowboy hat and boots had replaced the devil costume she'd given him, which I'd returned. She told the stories with fondness rather than criticism and seemed more focused on the pleasure Mark had given her through the years than the conflicts we'd worked through. I was happy for Lori to get a glimpse of Mark's childhood through Connie's devoted eyes.

It was pleasant to hear them in there together, reminiscing. I wish I'd had the chance, or taken the time, to imagine Connie as a young mother to Joel. Even a photo of them together would have served as a reminder that she wasn't born into this world as a mother-in-law, but as a little girl—and then a young woman, with hopes and dreams like me.

I wish Carl could have lived to enjoy this experience. But I'm pleased that Connie is still with us and has had the chance to see David, her great-grandchild. He won't remember her. But Lori and Mark are giving her some-thing nobody else can—a chance to hold a little bit of the future, a little of herself, in her arms.

October 12

I had a great talk with Diane this afternoon. She and Steven are planning a trip with Carolyn to spend Christmas in England! We caught up on family news and, since she hadn't mentioned her mother-in-law, I finally asked how things were going.

Diane seemed to collect her thoughts before answering.

"Well, if you talked to Mrs. Fleming, she'd probably say things are about the same as they've always been. But that isn't really true. She may not have changed, and she may not have noticed any changes in me. But my heart has changed. I finally realized that the anger and unforgiveness I was carrying around wasn't affecting her. It was only hurting me. I've been able to let go of that, and I feel much better about our relationship and my efforts in it, even though she doesn't seem to appreciate them."

She went on to say that I'd been a helpful, encouraging influence. "Your faith and persistence helped me, not just in my struggle with Mrs. Fleming, but in my marriage and my relationship with Carolyn. And," she added, "I'm asking some spiritual questions for the first time in my life. I appreciate your boldness with me, and your willingness to accept me just where I am." Our years as friends have provided us both with intimate times of sharing and many opportunities for growth. It's almost like having a sister. Thank you, God, for Diane.

October 24

Another generation has passed on. Connie died on her birthday, and although I'd heard of that happening before, it seemed strange when it happened to Connie, almost as if the time on her inner clock had simply run out. Lori and Joel and the baby had been here for lunch, and we'd celebrated her turning 78. She said goodbye to everyone and went to lie down just after we ate, saying she felt tired. Joel went into her room to check on her around dinnertime. Apparently she just died in her sleep. Her health had been especially bad these last few months, and the doctor had put her on some strong painkillers. I know Joel was aware of her decline, but still…I can't imagine not having parents. I thank God every day that Mom and Dad are doing so well.

There will be an empty space in my life as well as in my house from now on. Over these last years, Connie has become as much a figure in my day-to-day existence as any of my friends. As I think back over the years, I wonder if, given the chance, I'd have chosen Connie as a friend, or even as a family relative who became so involved in my life. But neither of us was given that choice. Husbands and wives choose each other. Daughters-in-law and mothers-in-law aren't allowed that privilege.

Still, she and I both matured in many ways since that first day when we met. I was young and impressionable and desperate for Joel's parents to like me. Connie was judgmental and opinionated and, I guess, a little insecure at having another woman in the house after raising three boys. For years it was all we could manage to be polite and civilized to one another. And look how far we've come.

Despite some trying days and occasional wounded egos, we've lived peacefully in the same home for the last two years. Though irritations are inevitable in relationships, it really helped once I was able to admit when I was wrong and ask Connie's forgiveness. New wounds could heal before they became irreparable scars. It took a decade for me to be able to humble myself before her. I wish I'd joined my women's Bible study group years sooner. I know I could never have taken that step without the encouragement of God's Word.

Maybe my willingness to admit being wrong served as an example to Connie, too. I remember the one time she apologized to me. After a big meal, during one of their visits, Carl and Joel began teasing me about a new haircut I'd just gotten. It was very short, and I didn't really like it myself. Joel started the teasing, playfully, and then Carl chimed in, and finally Connie agreed that it wasn't very becoming. From Connie, though, the criticism wasn't funny, and I started to cry. It seems silly now, and maybe it was just that time of the month or something. But my feelings were hurt. Later, when we were all in the kitchen cleaning up, she came and put an arm around me (very unlike her) and said, "I'm not very good with apologies, as you probably know by now. But I didn't mean to hurt your feelings by what I said. Forgive me?" She even told me about a permanent she once got that was so bad she didn't leave the house for days. Together, we had a good laugh. That apology meant everything to me. Even though there were other times I felt I deserved to hear the words "I'm sorry," I knew they were the two words Connie found most difficult to say. Forgiveness beca me easier for me, and the critical side of her seemed to show less and less often.

Connie finally came to an acceptance of who I am and who I'll never be. (Joel once told me that his mother fantasized that he would marry his high school sweetheart and that they'd run a successful business together!) I also came to terms with who Connie was—a very independent, old-fashioned woman who put her boys before everything and everyone else and did what she felt was best and right, even though it often didn't seem best or right to me. She was generous with Mark and loving towards Joel. She was a faithful wife to Carl for nearly fifty years. She voluntarily gave of her time and talents to those around her—including me—and many people cared for her.

Through the years, God provided the necessary grace for me to accept Connie and to constantly remember that she wasn't my mother and would never be able to give me the unconditional love and acceptance that only a parent can give. I just wish I'd been able to get to know her more private side a little better, if only to feel satisfied that she came to accept Christ as I always hoped she would. Not long ago, Mark told me that, following one of their afternoon visits, she asked him for a book about heaven. He was able to find one at a Christian bookstore. Maybe in her final season of life she was able to face the critical spiritual decisions that she'd put off for such a long time. I hope so, and I'm thankful that she felt close enough to

Mark to ask him such a tender question. It's funny—I worried so long and with such urgency about Connie's faith, and all along Mark was the one God planned to use to reach her.

It's impossible to put into words all that I've gained from my relationship with Joel's mother, and all the ways she touched my life. My prayer is that I'll be able to take from it everything that's good and pass these things along to Lori and Mark and David, as a mother-in-law, mother, and grandmother. The way Connie and I were finally able to love one another and eventually accept each other can only be attributed to the way God works in people who are willing to change and be changed. The things that have happened and the healing that took place in our relationship give me hope for growth and change in every other part of my life.

It's truly a miracle.

The End

Learning To Love

To actively pursue a better mother-in-law/daughter-in-law relationship, this study guide has been set up in eight sessions that are appropriate for individual or group study.

Although the questions are worded from the perspective of a daughter-in-law, the same questions are applicable to mothers-in-law by simply replacing the words "mother-in-law" with the words "daughter-in-law."

Study Guide
Schedule

You will find it more beneficial to work through the material as suggested in the Study Guide Schedule even if you are doing the study on your own. For group study, the books should be distributed and the assignment for Session One completed before the first meeting.

For Session One:

> Read the introduction (p. 3) and respond to the questionnaire for daughters-in-law (p. 7). Be honest. You do not have to share your answers. Answer the discussion questions for Session One (p. 77).

For Session Two:

> Take the Littauer Personality Test (p. 11). Answer the discussion questions for Session Two (p. 81).

For Session Three:

> Read "Living Out Love—A Journal" (p. 23). Answer the discussion questions for Session Three (p. 85).

For Session Four through Session Eight:

> Discussion questions will use the Bible as a reference. Any translation may be used but the New International Version is suggested. Be open to the truth God has for you.

Session One

1. Can you relate to the author's longing for "something more" in her relationship with her mother-in-law? Identify three areas that need improvement in your relationship.

2. Were there any questions on the questionnaire that were too difficult for you to answer? Which ones and why?

3. Would you describe your attitude after completing the questionnaire as hopeful or hopeless? Why?

4. Explain how your experiences as a daughter-in-law will help you become a more understanding mother-in-law.

5. Describe your husband's relationship with his mother. Do you think he desires a more loving relationship between you and his mother?

6. What is your standard approach to the problems you encounter in your life?

7. For the next eight weeks, can you make an effort to understand, accept, and even love your mother-in-law in a more vulnerable way? What if there is no response on her part?

LOVE IN ACTION:

Write a note to your mother-in-law expressing your desire for a closer relationship. If you feel comfortable doing so, mail it.

FOR FURTHER STUDY:

Irregular People by Joyce Landorf Heatherly.

Session Two

1. On the Littauer Personality Test, was it sometimes difficult to choose only one of the descriptive adjectives? Why? What helped you make the decision?

2. Were you surprised by your personality type? Would you have preferred another? Which one? Why?

3. What situations seem to magnify your undesirable personality traits? Do you often try to mask your natural reactions?

4. Describe some ways your personality affects your relationship with your mother-in-law. What do you think her personality type is? Is it compatible with yours?

5. List three strengths and three weaknesses of your personality.

6. Can you list three strengths and three weaknesses of your mother-in-law that might be attributed to her personality type?

7. How will this focus on personality help you to understand other important relationships?

LOVE IN ACTION:

Ask your mother-in-law to take the personality test. Compare your results.

FOR FURTHER STUDY:

Personality Plus by Florence Littauer.

Session Three

1. Could you determine the personality types of Mary Beth and Connie? How did personalities affect their relationship?

2. Disregarding the age difference, do you think that Mary Beth would have chosen Connie as a friend? Why or why not?

3. How would you describe Mary Beth's relationship with her mother? Joel's relationship with his mother?

4. Can you think of any instances in which Mary Beth felt inadequate as a wife and mother? Any in which she felt affirmed?

5. How did decisions regarding Mark intensify the struggle between Mary Beth and Connie? Was there a winner?

6. Describe any changes you detected in Mary Beth's attitude toward Connie as they both grew older. What do you think caused these?

7. In what ways could you relate to Mary Beth's story? Does a better relationship with your mother-in-law seem pure fantasy to you?

LOVE IN ACTION:

Using the pages at the back of this book, begin to keep a journal for the remaining weeks of this study.

FOR FURTHER STUDY:

Ordering Your Private World by Gordon McDonald (informative section on journaling).

Session Four

Theme verse: "We love because He first loved us." (1 John 4:19)

1. Read Mark 9:20–24 and James 4:8. Have you ever been in a situation—or relationship—that was beyond your control? What outside help did you seek? Have you ever asked God for help?

2. Read 2 Timothy 3:16 and Psalms 119:105. Do you consider the Bible to be a literary work, a history book, or the Word of God? What relevance does it have for you today?

3. Read John 3:16 and Jeremiah 29:11–13. Do you believe that God loves you? Does God care about the details of your life, such as your relationship with your mother-in-law?

4. Read Romans 3:22–25 and Romans 6:23. Can you be good enough to earn God's love? What hope has He provided for you?

5. Read 1 Peter 3:18 and John 14:6. Why was Christ's death part of God's plan for each of us?

6. Read John 3:1–5 and Romans 10:9–10. How do I receive the forgiveness and eternal life that Jesus offers?

7. Read 2 Corinthians 5:17 and 1 Peter 1:3–4. Will I be the same after I have asked Jesus to take control of my life?

LOVE IN ACTION:

Make the decision today to become God's child by genuinely offering this prayer: "Father, I'm sorry for my many sins against you and others. Thank you for the gift of forgiveness you provided for me through the death of your Son on the cross. Please come into my life and fill me with Your Holy Spirit. Amen.

FOR FURTHER STUDY:

More Than a Carpenter by Josh McDowell.

Session Five

Theme verse: "I will give you a new heart and put a new spirit in you." (Ezekiel 36:26)

1. Read 1 Samuel 16:7 and Psalms 44:21. What is God seeing when He looks at man? What is God seeing when He looks at your heart attitude toward your mother-in-law?

2. Read 1 Peter 1:22. How are we to love one another? When does this principle seem impossible to put into action?

3. Read John 5:19 and John 14:26. Where did Christ go for guidance? What help is available to us?

4. Read 1 John 4:7–21. Can you depend on Christ to fulfill your need to be loved? How will this affect the way in which you respond to rejection from your mother-in-law?

5. Read Romans 12:10. Use a dictionary to define "honor." If it seems impossible to love affectionately, can you love your mother-in-law by honoring her?

6. Read Colossians 3:12–15 and Romans 5:3–5. How do you "put on" love? Does this mean that your love is not genuine? Why or why not?

7. Read 1Corinthians 13:1–13. List the attributes of love that are given in this passage. Which aspect of love is the most difficult for you? Why?

LOVE IN ACTION:

Take the aspect of love that you chose as most difficult in the 1 Corinthians 13 passage. Substitute your name and your mother-in-law's name as follows: "Love is patient" becomes "Mary Beth is patient with Connie." Make this your prayer.

FOR FURTHER STUDY:

If by Amy Carmichael.

Session Six

Theme verse: "Do not conform any longer to the pattern of this world, but be transformed by the renewing of your mind." (Romans 12:2)

1. Read Romans 8:5–8. What is your mindset toward your mother-in-law? Do you think that it's pleasing to God?

2. Read 1 Peter 1:13–16. How are your thoughts related to your actions? How can we possibly "be holy, because God is holy"?

3. Read Jeremiah 31:33 and John 16:7–8, 13–14. What provisions did Jesus make for us before He left us? How can we expect to be affected?

4. Read Psalms 139:1–4, 23–24, and 1 John 1:8–9. Are you willing for God to search your thoughts and point out any offensive ways you have toward your mother-in-law? What will you do with these sins?

5. Read Proverbs 12:18–20, Ephesians 4:29–32, and James 1:19–20. List some of the words you often use to describe your mother-in-law. Are these words that build up and encourage?

6. Read Romans 12:3 and Philippians 2:3–4. In the past few weeks, have you had any changes of heart concerning your mother-in-law? What are some ways that you can reassure her of the important role she plays in both your and your husband's lives? If there are none, are you willing for that to change?

7. Read Philippians 4:6–8. Make a list of the things that worry you about your relationship with your mother-in-law. Make a list of anything that is excellent or praiseworthy.

LOVE IN ACTION:

Change the headings on the two lists you made in question #7 to "Requests" and "Thanksgivings." Present these to God in prayer this week. Record any reactions in your journal.

FOR FURTHER STUDY:

Lord, Change Me by Evelyn Christenson.

Session Seven

Theme verse: "Your attitude should be the same as that of Christ Jesus." (Philippians 2:5)

1. Read Matthew 11:28–30 and Philippians 2:5–11. What words are used to portray the attitude of Christ? Do any of these describe your attitude toward your mother-in-law?

2. Read Colossians 3:5–10 and Romans 8:13–14. Which of the behaviors listed do you need to "put to death"? What help is promised?

3. Read Colossians 3:12–14 and Romans 13:14. Are you willing to act in the ways taught even if you don't feel like it? Describe how it feels to be clothed in Christ.

4. Read Luke 6:37, Matthew 18:21–22, and Ephesians 4:31–32. Is there some incident involving your mother-in-law that you cannot seem to forget? Are you willing to forgive her? What if something similar happened again?

5. Read James 3:13–18. Would you rather be smart or wise? In control or submissive? Right or forgiving?

6. Read Galatians 5:16–25. Identify a sin that is present in your life. What would you like in its place?

7. Read Galatians 6:7–10. How can you continue doing good if you see no response or change in your mother-in-law? Have you prayed for her to become a part of the family of believers, if she is not one already, or thanked God if she is?

LOVE IN ACTION:

Sit down in a quiet place. Place an empty chair facing you and imagine your mother-in-law sitting there. Silently or aloud, ask her forgiveness for specific things which have hurt her, and offer your forgiveness for those incidences which have caused you pain. If it becomes too difficult, look to Christ, who is there with you, for the words to express what you're feeling.

FOR FURTHER STUDY:

Listening to Others by Joyce Huggett.

Session Eight

Theme verse: "Your people will be my people and your God my God." (Ruth 1:16)

1. Read Ruth 1:1–7. Do you think that Naomi was pleased with the wives her sons had chosen? Why or why not? What differences in your backgrounds have been obstacles in your relationship with your mother-in-law?

2. Read Ruth 1:8–15. When Naomi decided to return to her own land, was her release of her daughters-in-law an act of irresponsibility or love? Would you be relieved or hurt in a similar situation?

3. What qualities in Naomi could have caused her daughters-in-law to choose to leave their own family and land? How would you describe a "good" mother-in-law?

4. Read Ruth 1:16–22. What is Naomi's reaction to Ruth's demonstration of loyalty and love? What are some ways that you can demonstrate unconditional love toward your mother-in-law?

5. Read Ruth 2:1–23. List character traits of Ruth described in this chapter. What changes do you notice in Naomi? Reflect on any situation with your mother-in-law where you noticed a change when you chose to be loving.

6. Read Ruth 3:1–18. Can you imagine answering your mother-in-law as Ruth did in verse 5 of this chapter? Is it hard for you to even listen to her suggestions? What are some ways you could solicit her advice?

7. Read Ruth 4:1–22 and Matthew 1:1–6. What was the immediate blessing for Ruth? the greater blessing? Can you trust God with your situation, even if there is no blessing in sight?

LOVE IN ACTION:

Ask your mother-in-law to tell you about her relationship with her mother-in-law, using some of the topics mentioned on the questionnaire.

FOR FURTHER STUDY:

The Christian's Secret of a Happy Life by Hannah Whitall Smith.

Personal Journal

_____

_____

_____

_____

_____

_____

_____

_____

_____

_____

_____

_____

_____

_____

_____

_____

_____

_____

_____

_____

_____

_____

_____

"Your people will be my people,
and your God my God." (Ruth 1:16)

_____

_____

_____

_____

_____

_____

_____

_____

_____

_____

_____

_____

_____

_____

_____

_____

_____

_____

_____

_____

_____

_____

_____

_____

_____

_____

_____

_____

"Your attitude should be the same as that
of Christ Jesus." (Philippians 2:5)

"I will give you a new heart and put a new spirit in you."

(Ezekiel 36:26)

"We love because He first loved us." (1 John 4:19)

"Draw near to God, and He will draw near to you." (James 4:8)

_____

_____

_____

_____

_____

_____

_____

_____

_____

_____

_____

_____

_____

_____

_____

_____

_____

_____

_____

_____

_____

"Do not conform any longer
to the pattern of this world,
but be transformed by the renewing
of your mind." (Romans 12:2)